C000298986

Forward in

A Basic Lay Training Course
in the Ministry of Healing

St Albans Diocesan Group
for the Ministry of Healing

GROVE BOOKS LIMITED
RIDLEY HALL RD CAMBRIDGE CB3 9HU

Contents

Booklist

Ian Cowie, *Prayers and Ideas for Healing Services* (Wild Goose Publications, ISBN 0-947-98872-6): Session 6

John Gunstone, *The Lord is our Healer* (Hodder & Stoughton, ISBN 0-340-38462-X): Session 1

Benedict Heron, *Praying for Healing: The Challenge* (Darton, Longman & Todd, ISBN 0-232-51795-9): Sessions 1 and 6. Contains a number of testimonies.

Dennis & Matthew Linn, *Healing of Memories* (Paulist Press, ISBN 0-8091-1854-8): Session 4

Anne Long, *Listening* (Darton, Longman & Todd, ISBN 0-232-51834-6): Sessions 2 and 3

Francis MacNutt, *Healing* (Ave Maria, ISBN 0-87793-074-0): Sessions 1 and 3

Morris Maddox, *Twenty Questions on Healing* (SPCK, ISBN 0-281-04353-1): Session 1

Russ Parker, *Forgiveness is Healing* (Darton, Longman & Todd, ISBN 0-232-51960-9): Session 4

Mary Pytches, *Set My People Free* (Hodder & Stoughton, ISBN 0-340-40903-7): Session 4

Rosalind Rincker, *Prayer: Conversing with God* (Zondervan, ISBN 0-310-32092-5): Session 2

David Seamands, *Healing of Memories* (Victor, ISBN 0-946515-11-5): Session 4

Mark Stibbe, *Know your Spiritual Gifts* (Marshall Pickering, ISBN 0-551-03022-4): Session 5

Leo Thomas, *The Healing Team* (Paulist Press, ISBN 0-8091-2909-4): Sessions 3 and 6

John Wimber, *Power Healing* (Hodder & Stoughton, ISBN 0-340-39090-5): Session 5

The Cover Illustration is by the Group

First Impression December 1990
Reprinted July 1992
Revised Edition April 2000
Reprinted May 2004
ISSN 0144-171X
ISBN 1 85174 166 6

Preface

Carl Garner, Chairman,
St Albans Diocesan Group for the Ministry of Healing

Forward in Healing grew out of repeated requests from many parishes in St Albans Diocese to help them move forward in the healing ministry. They wanted to make three changes. Firstly, they wanted lay people to take part in this ministry, and not only the clergy. Secondly, they wanted to move from a fairly formal ministry with a reliance on set forms to something more personal. Thirdly, they wanted an openness to the gifts and guidance of the Spirit.

What was wanted and what we have produced is very much in line with the teaching of the 1988 Lambeth Conference.[1] The conference stressed that 'the ministry of healing should be a regular part of the ministry in every congregation.' It advised that since 'all the baptized and not only the clergy can be involved' there should be 'laying on of hands with prayer by the clergy *and* members of the congregation.' The bishops also recognized that the Holy Spirit gives some people 'special gifts of healing,' and urged each of us 'to enter increasingly into and to know in experience those gifts God has for him or her.' Such gifts are for the good of the church, and need to be fostered and monitored under its authority: 'the charismata of the Spirit are for the use and sharing of the whole church. In welcoming the gifts we emphasize the need for their exercise to be subject to the disciplines of the body of Christ.'

This course is an essentially practical one. The theological teaching that is part of each session is aimed at enabling people to experience what is being taught, rather than simply discussing it. Some preliminary study and discussion on the ministry of healing may often be advisable. The theology that lies behind the course is a dynamic one. It sees the ministry of healing not just as a response to a command, but as an entering further into the work of Christ.

In this ministry we seek to bring about a meeting between someone in need and the Lord who makes whole. To be of help in such an encounter demands a listening both to God and to the person. The approach followed tries to avoid the two extremes of ruling out the miraculous on one hand and denigrating the ordinary on the other. Hope is distinguished from presumption, and faith from credulity. Medical help and human care are esteemed, while the value of bringing everything to God in prayer is emphasized. The ministry of healing is a ministry of grace. We cannot guarantee the miraculous—but we can always be confident about the availability of grace, whatever form it may take.

---

1   The quotations are taken from *Mission and Ministry* paras 50–58 and 79–86. The italics are my own.

Introductory Notes

Purpose

This booklet contains the outline of a six-part course in the Christian ministry of healing. The course has been designed to meet an expressed need for some kind of basic training where there is a desire to involve lay people in this ministry in a personal way.

- It aims at broadening understanding, building confidence, fostering a capacity to listen and creating an ability to pray in a manner both positive and sensitive.
- It suggests areas of further exploration in this ministry.
- It is primarily a training course, not a study course.
- It needs commitment by participants to attending the whole course.
- The last session deals with deciding what is appropriate in the local setting.

Use

This booklet is intended for leaders and provides the outlines they will need for conducting a session. These are found under the headings: Aim, Worship, Teaching, Testimony, Workshop and Conclusion.

Worship

Each session should start with worship. Suitable hymns and songs are suggested, together with a collect and a Scripture reading (MCP = *Mission Praise,* Combined Edition, 1990; SOFC = *Songs of Fellowship,* Combined Edition, 1991; AMR = *Ancient & Modern,* Revised). CW refers to the new Common Worship.

Teaching

Under this heading are found key theological and practical points with which the leader should be conversant. It could be presented in a variety of ways.

There may be times when preparatory reading is advisable. A select booklist has been provided on page 2 above.

Testimony

Testimonies appropriate to each session are provided. A relevant local testimony given in person would be preferable.

Workshop

The workshop is central to the course. Each workshop group should comprise 5 to 8 people, and have a leader to start it off and keep it on course. A summary of teaching is provided for such leaders.

Session 1: The Mandate

Aim

To communicate to the participants that the mandate to 'heal the sick' (Luke 10.9) is still addressed to the church, and is primarily fulfilled through prayer.

Introduction

Explanation of the nature and purpose of the course. Welcome.

Worship

Seek ye first	MPC 590, SOFC 493
O for a thousand tongues	AMR 196, MPC 496, SOFC 412
Praise, my soul	AMR 365, MPC 560, SOFC 466
Take my life, and let it be	AMR 361, MPC 624, SOFC 519
Yesterday, today, for ever	MPC 787
Dear Lord and Father of mankind	AMR 184, MPC 111, SOFC 79
Praise You, Lord	MPC 565, SOFC 472
Glorious things of Thee are spoken	AMR 257, MPC 173, SOFC 127

Reading: Matt 9.35–38.

Prayer: Collect for 2nd Sunday before Lent, *ASB* p 490.
(3rd Sunday before Advent, CW.)

The Lord's Prayer.

Teaching

Healing in the Ministry of Jesus

'And many followed him, and he healed them all' (Matt 12.15). The gospels are full of accounts of Jesus healing the sick. There are individual stories: the centurion's servant (Matt 8.5–13); the ten lepers (Lk 17.11–19); the man with a withered arm in the synagogue (Mk 3.1–5); the paralytic lowered through the roof (Mk 2.1–12); the woman with a haemorrhage (Mk 5.25–34); the deaf and dumb man (Mk 7.31–35); the blind man at the pool of Bethesda (Jn 5.1–13); and many more. In some passages the sheer number of people healed by Jesus is remarked upon. Clearly healing was an important part of his ministry. No wonder the crowd remarked, 'he has done all things well, he has made the blind to see and the lame to walk' (Mk 7.37). Healing and the proclamation of the gospel go hand in hand in the ministry of our Lord.

Healing in the Ministry of the Apostles

Healing was not limited to our Lord alone. Jesus commissioned his apostles to share in his ministry, and the mandate they were given included both the preaching of the gospel and the healing of the sick. The command to preach the gospel is very clear after our Lord's resurrection, 'Go out into all the world, preach the gospel to all peoples' (Mk 16.15).

What of the command to heal? All the evidence is that it too remains in force, and that the commission to 'obey all that I commanded you' (Matt 28.20) includes the ministry of healing.

After our Lord's ascension, and the sending of the Spirit, the apostles did not cease this ministry, but continued it. The quasi-canonical ending to Mark's gospel clearly envisages the continuance of the ministry within the church: 'these signs shall follow those who believe, they shall work wonders…they shall speak in other tongues…they shall lay their hands upon the sick who will recover' (Mk 16.15–18).

In John's gospel, Jesus teaches the apostles to expect that when the Spirit comes the church will continue to do such things: 'the works I do you will do also, and greater things you shall do because I go to the Father' (Jn 14.12). When the Spirit came these words came true: thousands were converted, and the Acts of the Apostles records many instances where the apostles healed in the name of Jesus. Peter heals the lame man at the beautiful gate of the temple in the name of Jesus; Paul heals the lame man in Lystra (Acts 14). Nor was it only the twelve; Philip, a deacon, preaches and heals in Samaria (Acts 8.4–7) and Paul himself was healed by Ananias, who seems to have been a layman (Acts 9.17). The whole church prays that God would give boldness to the apostles to preach the Word, and that he would stretch forth his hand to heal and work wonders (Acts 4.30).

A Continued Mandate?

The belief that the command to heal in the name of Jesus is only applicable to the apostles, or to the time of the apostles, has no foundation in Scripture, nor is it supported by history. In the early centuries of the church there are numerous references to healings taking place. Authorized forms for laying hands on the sick and for anointing them with oil are present from the earliest times, based both on apostolic precedent (Mk 6.13) and on the clear authority of James (James 5.18ff). Why then did the belief arise, particularly at the Reformation, that the ministry of healing was only for the time of the apostles? Three reasons may be adduced: (1) The authorized forms of service were only being used for the dying; (2) the Reformers had personally come across no healings; (3) any healings claimed were mixed up with superstition, and to admit them would damage their case. To these reasons must be added the doubt that healings ever could happen—or ever did.

An Impossible Mandate?

Is the mandate to 'heal the sick' an impossible one therefore? James talks of the 'prayer of faith' healing the sick, which means it is not just the outward gestures which are significant. It also draws attention to the promises about prayer made by Jesus: 'whatever you ask in my name will be done for you' (John 15.16); 'whatever you ask for, believing, you will obtain' (Mark 11.24); 'where two or three of you on earth agree about anything you ask for, it will be done for you'

(Matt 18.20). It would be possible to dismiss such promises as untrue, or as tauto-logical ('If you ask for what you are going to receive you will receive it'). There is another way, which is to see them as based on the actual experience of Jesus and as invitations to us to begin to enter into their truth. After all, even the apostles were not always able to fulfil the Lord's command (Matt 17.16). Our Lord himself was not able to 'do any great work' at Nazareth, because of the people's lack of faith (Mk 6.5–6). Moreover, on one occasion the healing that occurred was not absolutely immediate—when he healed the blind man who first saw people walk-ing like trees (Mk 8.22–25).

It follows from what has been said that two extremes need to be avoided: the unfaithful pessimism that thinks nothing astounding can ever happen; and the presumptuous optimism that thinks if we get the formula right, the miraculous must always happen.

The ministry of healing is not an alternative to medical care, nor is it in oppo-sition to it. God can use our prayers in many ways, including blessing the work of doctors and nurses and others involved in the healing professions. Sometimes it seems our prayers limit the side-effects of treatment, at other times they will seem to assist recuperation. Sometimes the miraculous will occur. On many occa-sions people will find a new or renewed faith, and a strength to go on. We do not know all the answers, but we can grow in faith and become more effective in prayer and learn to be better channels for the grace of God.

In the Name of Jesus

What is important about the church's ministry of healing, and what is distinc-tive about it, is that it is done in the name of Jesus. It witnesses to him and conse-quently it is an ally of the gospel. The ministry of healing provides a potent avenue for people to recognize and accept that fundamental healing which is at the heart of the gospel—the healing that can always be assured through repentance and faith, the healing of our relationship with God, the healing of the cross. It is for this reason that dramatic healings in the New Testament are so often called 'signs'; they point beyond themselves to Christ. They also confirm the truth of the gos-pel—'and God confirmed the word they spoke with signs and wonders and gifts of the Holy Spirit' (Heb 2.4).

The ministry of healing is a journey of discovery and it is a journey of prayer. It starts where all Christian ministry begins—with repentance, with faith in Christ, and with prayer for the Holy Spirit. God may—God will—surprise us, as we enter on this pilgrimage in fulfilment of our Lord's command to 'heal the sick.'

Testimony

The testimony is of a healing witnessing to the possibility of the 'miraculous.' David had broken his ankle, but that had been some time ago, and as far as he could tell it had healed completely. Then he started getting pains. He sought medical advice and was told that he had arthritis, and was advised to give up sport, advice he was unwilling to take. The pain got worse, and he was forced to give up sport. He then attended a meeting at his church in which he was challenged to reach out to God. As he tried to do this he seemed to hear God saying he should jump off a chair on to his sore ankles: 'It was a crazy thing to do but I did it.' To his surprise he felt no pain. Nor was the pain there when he resumed sport: 'I could move with a freedom I hadn't known for years.' Some time later however some pain did recur—only to go again after an inner battle of faith.

Workshop

Break into groups. The task for each group is (1) for everyone to introduce themselves, (2) to discuss what has been taught, and (3) to prepare comments and questions. The group leader begins the discussion by referring to the aim of the session and by summarizing the teaching.

Summary of Teaching

- The apostolic church continues the ministry.
- Healings and forms of service for healing continue through later centuries.
- Reasons for Reformation scruples and modern doubts.
- A venture in prayer: entering into Christ's promises.
- Avoiding 'faithless pessimism' and 'presumptuous optimism.'
- Not an alternative to medicine.
- Done in Jesus' name.
- Points to the healing in Christ.
- Starts with repentance and faith, and prayer for the Spirit.

The comments and questions are then dealt with in plenary.

Conclusion

An act of commitment to Christ, and to the ministry of healing, together with a prayer for the outpouring of the Spirit, perhaps as follows:

Leader: The Christian ministry of healing begins where all Christian ministry begins, in repentance, in faith in Christ, and in prayer for the Spirit. Therefore I ask you, in the name of the living God who came to us in his Son:

Do you repent of your sins?

R   **I do.**

Leader: Do you believe in Jesus?

R   **I do.**

Leader: Do you desire to move forward in the ministry of healing, with the help of the Holy Spirit?

R   **I do.**

Leader: Let us pray:

> Heavenly Father and everlasting God, anointed by your Spirit, your Son our Lord Jesus Christ preached the gospel and healed the sick. Fill these your servants who believe in your Word with the Holy Spirit. Empower them for your service. Pour upon them your Spirit of love and joy and peace. Anoint them with the Spirit of Jesus, in whom alone we find both healing and salvation, and in whose name we ask. Amen.

This could be done with laying on of hands. If the group is large, hands could be held during the prayer, and during a short period afterwards while each person prays silently for their neighbours on either side.

The Grace.

Session 2: Channels of Grace

Aim

To help us understand the importance of prayer for the ministry of healing, and to learn how to pray supportively in small groups, so as to be better channels of grace.

Worship

Thou, Lord, hast given Thyself for our healing	MPC 698
There is a redeemer	MPC 673, SOFC 544
Bind us together	MPC 54, SOFC 43
Make me a channel of your peace	MPC 456, SOFC 381
In the name of Jesus	MPC 339, SOFC(2) 818.
Breathe on me breath of God	AMR 236, MPC 67, SOFC 51
All earth was dark	MPC 8
Peace is flowing like a river	MPC 554, SOFC 458
Love divine	AMR 205, MPC 449, SOFC 377
O Holy Spirit	AMR 231

Reading: Matt 18.19–20.

Prayer: *ASB* p 105 section 9.

The Lord's Prayer.

Teaching

A Shared Ministry

The church today is being stirred to expect great things from God as it learns to attempt great things for him—and that must include healing of body, mind and spirit. However, as soon as a church becomes aware of the potential for a pastoral ministry of healing, the question arises as to who should be involved. Is it a ministry that should be restricted to the ordained?

Jesus shared his own ministry of healing with the twelve apostles, and a little later a further seventy-two were also sent out (Lk 10.1). Paul mentions those with a gift of healing separately from apostles, prophets and teachers (1 Cor 12.28). Ananias, who laid hands on Paul so that he 'might see again and be filled with the Spirit,' is simply described as 'a Christian' (Acts 9.10). James mentions that the sick should call for the elders of the church to pray over them and anoint them in the name of the Lord, but he goes on to say that we should all 'pray for one another, that we may be healed' (Jas 5.16).

Through prayer we all share in the ministry of healing. God can use our prayer, however imperfect it may be. We may have been used to praying from a list of prayers for the sick—perhaps on our own (after Jesus' example of withdrawing to a quiet place), or in church (Jesus also went regularly to the synagogue to pray). But we can go further. The way to do so is through learning to pray in a group.

The Prayer Group

Jesus recommended prayer in groups, and he attached promises to it:

'Where two of you on earth agree about anything you pray for, it will be done for you...for where two or three come together in my name, I am there with them.'   Matthew 18.19–20

The apostles—that group of twelve men Jesus gathered together at the time of his ministry—would have understood what Jesus was trying to say. They were his companions. Within this group setting they travelled with Jesus, listened to him, questioned him, and saw him at work. Sometimes he would go aside with two or three of them in order to pray. So, both in a larger group or in a smaller one, they learnt from him, and began to carry out the same healing work.

So too for us. In a group we learn to pray and be prayed for. We are encouraged and supported. We grow in Christian knowledge and discover and use gifts. The group becomes a training ground for a more public ministry of healing. As a ministry team develops, it will need to meet together for teaching and prayer, and smaller groups within such a team will need to prayer together before any healing service or ministry, as well as during it.

The Point of Prayer in Groups

Perhaps you may in the past have experienced some problems in prayer groups:
• Total silence...heads down, eyes tightly shut: too overcome with embarrassment to be able to pray aloud.
• Not knowing what to say. Afraid of not being able to express it properly. Frightened of being asked to pray.
• Afraid of being shown up, of appearing too spiritual, or not spiritual enough.
• Prayers are prayed, but they are like disconnected spiritual shopping lists.
• Something important is mentioned, and then ignored by the rest.
• Only one person prays...at length.
• Keeping things close to the chest, not trusting others.
• Talking outside about things that should have been kept private.
• Pretentious prayers couched in unintelligible language.
• Being 'preached at' when people say what they think under the guise of prayer.
• A social get-together with a prayer tacked on the end.

Things go wrong when the reasons for having a prayer group are forgotten. A prayer group is not a meditation group, it is not a discussion group, it is not an alternative worship group, it is not a setting for a private prayer time.

There are two main reasons for having a prayer group:
1. To enter into the promise made by Jesus to two or three agreeing in prayer.
2. To be a school for prayer-ministry.

How Can We Pray 'In agreement'?

Matthew 18.19: 'If two of you on earth agree about anything you pray for, it will be done for you.' In many of the instances quoted of what can go wrong with a prayer group, 'agreement' is not actually the word that springs to mind. How can we pray in agreement? Here are some suggestions:

1. *Pray Aloud.* If a request for prayer is only met by silence, how does the person we pray with know we have been listening? Silence is valuable, but it does not express concern just of itself. The first step towards praying in agreement is to *pray aloud.* Jesus prayed aloud. There are many examples of this in the gospels. We would never have known what Jesus prayed otherwise.

2. *Pray Supportively.* The second step is to pray supportively. Instead of wondering what you are going to say, come prepared to *listen* and to *support.* Put into words of prayer what has been mentioned. Others—at least two or three—then pick up the request and put it into their own words. Yet others may then pick up from there. We want those for whom we are praying to know we care enough to pray.

3. *Pray Simply.* When you pray be natural with God. Tell him what you really feel, in your own words. Do not think you have to match the words of the liturgy, or speak perfect prose. Pray as you would usually speak, simply and conversationally, but addressed to God. Do not pray at great length. If a new insight comes to you, introduce it later after giving others a chance to pray.

Channels of Grace

As we learn to pray in agreement, we will become better able to communicate love through prayer. Not just our love and concern, but God's love in Christ. We will become real channels of grace.

Testimony

The testimony is one of a healing through prayer in a group. Margaret had a swelling in her neck which her doctor diagnosed as a growth on her thyroid gland. She was told the only treatment for it was by surgery. She felt unhappy about this, and before making up her mind, asked for prayer and the laying on of hands from a church healing group. On return to her doctor to hear about the result of some tests, it was discovered that the lump had noticeably decreased in size. The doctor rightly warned her against being too optimistic, yet a fortnight later the lump had dissipated completely, and has not recurred. Margaret gives thanks to Jesus for his love and for healing her through the prayers of the group.

Workshop

1. *In plenary:* Ask everybody to think for a moment of one thing that has made them glad, and one thing that has made them sad. Pair off. Each person relates in turn the thing that has made them glad. They then repeat back to the other person what they have heard. Then ask them to put what the other person said into a simple prayer of thanksgiving, 'Thank you God that...' Remind them that at this point it is only about what has made them glad.

2. *Divide into groups:* Allow a short time for renewal of personal introductions. Refer to the aim of the session and run briefly over the main points of the teaching. Do not ask for prayer requests. Have a short period of silence for people to recollect God's presence and to ask silently to be channels for his love. Then begin praying, reminding them that they have already thought of 'something sad.' If it looks like becoming a discussion, the leader ensures that people pray by gently saying 'let's turn that into a prayer.'

Summary of Teaching

- A ministry in which we already share through prayer.
- Going further through a prayer group.
- Problems with prayer groups.
- Reasons for a prayer group:
  (a) To enter into the promise regarding agreement.
  (b) To be a school for prayer-ministry.
- How to pray 'in agreement':
  (1) Pray aloud.
  (2) Pray supportively.
  (3) Pray simply and conversationally.

3. *Ask for reactions* afterwards, in plenary.
   Closing prayer:
   Lord, you have taught us that when two or three are gathered together in your name you are there in our midst. Help us to be ever conscious of your presence and to be ever more effective channels of your grace. Amen.

   The Grace.

Session 3: A Definite Touch

Aim

To encourage the participants to pray in a positive way for people with physical ailments and other obvious personal needs, using word and touch in the name of Jesus.

Worship

As we are gathered, Jesus is here	MPC 38, SOFC 28
Be still and know	MPC 48, SOFC 41
How sweet the name of Jesus sounds	AMR 192, MPC 251, SOFC 194
On Jordan's bank	AMR 50, MPC 538
Praise, my soul, the King of Heaven	AMR 365, MPC 560, SOFC 466
Reach out and touch the Lord	MPC 569
Thou whose almighty word	AMR 266, MPC 699, SOFC 557
When I feel the touch	MPC 753, SOFC 594

Reading: Mark 8.22–25.

Prayer: Collect for the Sunday after Christmas, *ASB* p 450 (also CW).

Lord's Prayer.

Teaching
Incarnational Healing

God, who created and cares about this material and physical universe, came to us in Jesus Christ: 'The Word was made flesh and dwelt among us' (John 1.14). In his coming amongst us in Jesus, God came to us in a definite and physical way. 'The fullness of the Godhead dwelt bodily in him' (Col 2.9). The invisible God was made manifest in human form. So John can write:

'We write to you about the Word of life, which has existed from the very beginning. We have heard it. We have seen it with our eyes: yes, we have seen it, and our hands have touched it…'　　　　1 John 1.1

In his earthly ministry this tangibility runs through all that Jesus is and does. Thus it is present in his ministry of healing. He reaches out to people with word and gesture in a definite and positive manner. For example:

Gestures:
a) The deaf and dumb man—Jesus puts his fingers in his ears, and touches his tongue (Mk 7.32–37)
b) The blind man anointed with clay and spittle (Jn 9.1–12)
c) Laying on of hands: 'He laid hands on the sick and they recovered' (Lk 4.40)

14

Word:

a) The paralytic: 'Be of good cheer, your sins are forgiven you…' (Mk 2.1–12)
b) The ten lepers: 'I will, be clean.' (Mk 2.41)
c) Blind Bartimaeus: 'Go, your faith has healed you' (Mk 10.46–52)

Contact, symbolism, personal words all have their place. Touch, which may have such a natural healing power, and which can help to communicate our human love and concern, is used by Jesus to convey the love and healing of the God who made us all. The ministry of healing is incarnational.

On their part, people sought contact with Jesus. The sick reached out to him, like the woman with a haemorrhage (Lk 8.43f), wanting 'at least to touch the edge of his cloak' (Mk 6.56). They came to him that they might hear him and be healed by him and 'all the people tried to touch him, for power was going out from him and healing them all' (Lk 6.19).

Within the Church

Christ who died and rose again with our human nature is present now within his church by his Spirit. He is the same Lord with the same compassion, and the same power to save and heal. The church is his body, the special instrument of his will. As the apostles bore witness to the resurrection, so God's grace was present in abundance. Through word and gesture they healed the sick—yet it was not them, but Christ. They were used by God to help bring about a meeting between the Lord and those who turned to him. They helped people to 'reach out and touch the Lord.' They laid on hands, as their Lord did, and his power flowed through them, and his hands touched those who sought him. Of all the gestures mentioned, the laying on of hands is one of the simplest, and yet one of the most profound. We too can be the hands of Christ. We too can be alongside others helping them to reach out to him. Jesus Christ is alive, the church is still his body, and his Spirit which he poured out on his church has not been called back.

Starting to Minister

As we start to minister in prayer to those who seek it, we try and assist them to 'reach out and touch the Lord':

a) *Listening to them:* Asking them their name, and what it is they would like prayer for.
b) *Inviting faith:* Do they believe in Jesus? Explain that we are accompanying them to the 'throne of grace.'
c) *Focusing on Jesus:* Suggest that they picture him while you are praying, or that they silently repeat a prayer of faith.

We then pray 'in agreement': simply, conversationally, supportively. We pray using their name. And we pray directly and positively.

Praying Positively

Pray on the basis of Scripture. Hold before God some of the reasons why we can presume to pray. The Collects do this: 'O God you are/have said/promise... therefore...' God's promises are mentioned, or something he has done, or an attribute he possesses, as the grounds for praying about a present request. 'Remember, Lord...' If there is a biblical story that seems to fit the situation, it could be read, and then prayers based upon it.

Pray with compassionate understanding. Try and envisage what the person's problem means to them. Who else needs praying for? Family? Doctor? Nurses? Does it making shopping difficult, for instance? Be ready to ask.

Pray according to your measure of faith: the magnitude of a physical illness may be so great that you find it hard to believe that God could heal it, and harder to believe he could use you. In this case, break the problem down. Pray about it bit by bit. If there are a number of symptoms, pray about them one by one.

Pray making use of the imagination. Visualise what you are praying in your mind's eye. See the person getting better, or even fully restored, or the wound healing, or the joint moving. Visualise Christ laying his hands on the person, or his love and light bathing them.

Pray making use of touch. Lay hands lightly upon the persons head and shoulders. If they are seated perhaps hold their hands. If appropriate, a hand may be placed over the area of pain, or extended towards it.

Comments and Cautions
- Do not be perturbed by tears.
- Do not be worried either by the presence of sensations of heat or 'electricity' as you lay on hands, nor by their absence. Such experiences may however indicate the length of time you should go on praying—until they seem to cease. If someone expresses hesitancy about having hands laid on them, or even to having their hands held, respect this. It may be appropriate to arrange for further prayer and counselling.
- Do not suggest that someone receiving medication dispenses with it because they seem to feel better. Tell them to see the doctor.
- Never condemn. Never suggest that if someone who has desired healing has not apparently received it, it must be due to their lack of faith. Do not recommend that people pretend they are healed when they are not. Encourage honesty and thanksgiving for God's love and the measure of grace that has been received.

Testimony

The testimony is one of physical healing. Gina was injured in a train crash when she was a teenager. She had several operations on one of her legs which had been badly broken. Her walking was very limited and her leg was very painful. She also had severe headaches. Osteomyelitis was subsequently diagnosed. Gina began a journey of faith which led to a desire that Jesus should be Lord of her life. She was introduced to a Christian lay person with a particular gift of healing, who laid hands on her and prayed silently for quite some time. Gina first felt cold, and then 'warmth flooded through the whole of me…though my eyes were closed the room seemed full of sunlight.'

'Afterwards I felt an incredible sense of peace, as if all sorts of knots I hadn't even known were inside me had been untied.' Her headaches went and the pain and swelling in her legs. She began to walk long distances. Although she cannot run, she regards what has happened as marvellous. The healing she received was not only physical, but also healing from fears and hurtful memories of the past.

Workshop

Break into groups. Mention the aim of the session and briefly summarise the main points of the teaching. Emphasize this is not a discussion group. Suggest a period of silence for people to call to mind ailments or concerns they have. Mention the possibility of 'standing proxy.' Afterwards leader asks how it went.

Summary of Teaching

Christ's ministry of healing involved the tangible—he used human gestures and words to communicate God's love. By his Spirit he is present in his church. We are his body. As we start to minister in prayer to those who seek it, we try and assist them to 'reach out and touch the Lord':

- Listening to name and need.
- Inviting faith in Jesus.
- Suggesting they visualise Jesus or use a prayer of faith.
- Pray 'in agreement'—simply, conversationally, supportively.
- Pray directly and positively.
- Pray on the basis of Scripture.
- Pray with compassionate understanding.
- Pray according to your measure of faith.
- Pray making use of the imagination.
- Pray making use of touch.

Allow a short time for comments in plenary.

Conclusion

Almighty God, and everlasting Father, your Son, our Saviour Jesus Christ, conveyed your love in healing touch and word. Grant us, the members of his church, such a measure of your grace, that through our prayers and ministry the sick in body, soul, or mind, may meet the healer of the world, even Jesus Christ our Lord.

A blessing (*ASB* p 107) or the Grace.

Session 4: Going Deeper

Aim

To introduce the participants to teaching and experience of inner healing.

Worship

Jesus, the Name high over all	MPC 385, SOFC 307
Jesus, we enthrone you	MPC 388, SOFC 310
Do not be afraid	MPC 115
Jesus, name above all names	MPC 375, SOFC 298
O let the Son of God enfold you	MPC 502, SOFC 419
Jesu, lover of my soul	AMR 193, MPC 372, SOFC 297
O love that will not let me go	AMR 359, MPC 515, SOFC 434
Dear Lord and Father of mankind	AMR 184, MPC 111, SOFC 79
Peace, perfect peace	AMR 358, MPC 555, SOFC 977

Reading: John 21.1–9, 15–19.

Prayer: Collect for 7th Sunday before Easter, *ASB* p 495
(also CW 21st Sunday after Trinity).

Lord's Prayer.

Teaching

The Biblical Basis for Inner Healing

'Peace is what I leave with you; it is my own peace that I give you. I do not give it as the world does. Do not be worried and upset; do not be afraid' (Jn 14.27). An important part of the salvation Jesus came to teach and demonstrate was *shalom*, meaning peace, wholeness or harmony at every level. This peace comes from the experience of sins forgiven, and of a right relationship with God that comes from genuine repentance and real commitment to Jesus Christ. It comes also as fear and anxiety are driven from us. It comes when our inner burdens are taken by God, when self-hate and despair are replaced by God with thoughts that are 'good and true and holy.' God is love and his concern is for our healing (Ex 15.26). Salvation is about wholeness and healing which can touch our bodies, minds and spirits. It is about the 'peace of God which passes all understanding guarding our hearts and minds through Christ Jesus' (Phil 4.7).

The Need for Inner Healing

We are all damaged people in need of healing—this is part of the effects of sin. In a fallen world no-one escapes. But some have been so damaged by events in the earlier stages of their lives that they are left vulnerable and bewildered. Others have been traumatized by what has happened to them more recently, and are deeply hurt within. The causes of all such inner distress are manifold:

18

- Premature separation from a parent through sickness, divorce or death, which can be experienced as a rejection.
- Experience of failure (perhaps at school).
- Experiences of overwhelming fear.
- Experience of abuse—mental, physical, sexual, often resulting in fear, guilt and shame.
- A family history of psychological problems (alcoholism, violence, involvement in the occult).
- Personal experimenting with drugs, alcohol abuse or dabbling in the occult.
- Experience of abortion.
- Inability to grieve in bereavement.
- Any persistent, unresolved burden of guilt.

Often such incidents or memories are pushed down below our conscious thinking where they remain, unseen but felt sometimes in debilitating ways.

Symptoms of the need for inner healing can include fear, anger, anxiety, resentment, self-hatred, guilt, unforgiveness, an inability to trust, persistent irrational beliefs ('I'm no good,' 'I can't get it right').

The good news is that Jesus is Lord of time (Matt 28.20). He cannot alter the facts of the past but he can and does heal the effects of them so that our present and future can be lived differently. If there are parts of our past which continue to hurt, distort, spoil our present, God will come in to touch, forgive, free, heal and renew us as we open up to him.

The Importance of Forgiveness

An important part of inner healing is forgiveness. The hurt person not only needs to forgive the one(s) who hurt him or her (Matt 18.21–25) but also to confess and receive forgiveness for any hurts caused as a natural but sinful reaction to being hurt. It can be very difficult to forgive if the hurt is deep. It may not be possible or even desirable for a relationship to be restored, but what is essential is that the hurt person is set free from resentment, and in turn 'releases' the person who has hurt them. Here the love, faith and prayer of those ministering will help, especially if the hurt person feels they want to forgive but cannot yet do so. Resentment (the need to forgive) and guilt (the need to be forgiven) are like bits of grit in a deep physical wound. Once washed out, healing can follow but if the grit remains it can lead to secondary infection. So, in the Spirit, the combined presence of resentment and guilt leaves the person more vulnerable to the attack of the enemy and secondary effects, such as fear. Inner healing may be appropriate for a person suffering from fears, phobias, or compulsions.

Essential to any form of inner healing are a willingness:

- To be honest;
- To be open to God and turn to him in repentance;
- To receive forgiveness;
- To forgive both others and oneself.

The Developed Ministry

The developed ministry of inner healing demands time, perhaps one or two hours, and often more than one session. It needs an undisturbed and comfortable setting. It calls for considerable attentiveness to the person and to God. Prayer must permeate the whole session. It can follow a pattern something like this:

a) 'We are going to ask the Holy Spirit to come and bring to light anything he wants to deal with. So relax and be open to God. Share with us any thoughts, feelings, memories or pictures that come to you.'

b) Some people may go quickly to an event or place in their past, others may be silent for a time. If a visual memory comes, the person is asked to describe it as they see it.

c) At the right point (but not prematurely) the Lord is asked to come and heal. The person may well sense the presence of Jesus with them. It is important not to 'stage manage' but to let the Lord come as he chooses.

d) If the person is stuck, questions like 'What is happening to you now?' or 'Are you aware of feeling or thinking anything?' may be asked.

e) What happens may be quite surprising, as the person begins to experience God's love and healing touch the sore points in their memory, and his peace sinks deeper into them. They may tangibly 'feel' this happening, or the memory may just seem to fade and lose its sting, or Christ may vividly present himself to their imagination in a healing way.

f) The person is encouraged to speak to the Lord and to listen to what he says. At this stage those ministering are often quietly in prayer—though it may be with their eyes open to watch the person's reactions.

g) An awareness of personal sin and real guilt may also arise, with sorrow, and as these are admitted, prayer for forgiveness is made, and words of assurance given.

h) After prayer, consideration is given to further ministry, or any 'homework' that may be necessary—making acts of affirmation of worth in God's eyes, permitting the Holy Spirit to renew patterns of thought.

Where Do We Start?

Perhaps all this sounds rather daunting, and not where we are at the moment. But we can begin. Indeed, we have to begin. Many who come forward for prayer in a healing service want help in trouble, strength to face life, or wisdom to make a right decision. Even those who ask prayer for physical illnesses may be more concerned with other issues. Listening sympathetically may indicate what is not put into so many words. The following may be helpful as we begin to minister inner healing:

1. Encourage the person to come with their burden to the foot of the cross, seeing it with their mind's eye.

2. Encourage them to make an act of forgiveness of those who have hurt them.

As each such person comes to mind they could say aloud 'Lord Jesus, in your name and for your sake I forgive N...' If they cannot do this, pray that they will be given the grace to become able to do so.

3. Pray for God's peace to suffuse and hold them.
4. Read or quote assuring passages of the Bible.
5. Continue praying in silence.
6. Arrange for further ministry as appropriate or feasible—confession, sessions for inner healing in greater depth, or short sessions of 'soaking prayer' on a regular basis, perhaps weekly.

Comments and Cautions

- Confidentiality is crucial in all levels of this ministry. Any private matter should be regarded as being under the 'seal of the confessional', not to be talked about with anyone afterwards (not even the praying team) unless raised or requested or allowed by the person him- or herself.
- Do not try and give 'instant advice.'
- Do not be over-concerned about the person's reactions, whether expressions of feelings like tears or cries, or by people 'relaxing' into a chair or subsiding onto the floor. Neither be put off by apparent lack of reaction.
- Do be aware of long-standing conditions, where medical or other professional help may be needed. Do not work against help being received.

Testimony

The testimony is one of inner healing. Sarah grew up feeling unwanted. Her birth, as the second of unsuspected twins, caught her parents unprepared. Her father seemed unable to express his love, her mother's love was perceived as conditional and she felt like a possession rather than a person. As the youngest, Sarah felt 'put down' by the family, and critical schoolteachers strengthened this feeling.

Sarah was never comfortable with men, and two close relationships ended disastrously. Female friendships suffered from her own critical attitude, reinforcing her feelings of isolation, guilt and rejection. In her late 30s she changed career, but her low self-confidence meant she was ill-equipped her to handle her responsibilities and the attitudes of some colleagues.

She came for ministry in despair and depression, but soon accepted that she must unreservedly forgive and cease to blame (consciously or unconsciously) people who had hurt her, repenting of her own long-standing unforgiveness.

This, with an increasing understanding of God's unconditional love for her, dramatically changed her attitude to life and to her parents. Her confidence at work improved greatly, and she copes adequately. She can also cope with the times of feeling unwanted which still recur.

Workshop
a) Start by simply reminding each other of your names.
b) In the group, but in silence, reflect on your day—events, people, relationships. Be open to God's perspective. Become aware of any points of tension, stress, resentment, jealousy, anger. Let God bring these to mind rather than yourself stirring things up. Now, in the silence, let the Lord come to you. What does he want to say to you? What do you want to say to him?
c) Afterwards ask whether anyone has a request for prayer following on from this, or from the teaching. Listen to the person. Listen to God as to how to pray. Then pray for them as suggested (see summary of teaching), aloud and in silence, as a group.

Summary of Teaching

Christ's salvation brings peace. This not only comes with the forgiveness of sins but also with inner healing. Some greatly need the healing of Christ's peace because of what they have experienced in life.

Essential to any form of inner healing are a willingness:

• To be honest;
• To be open to God and turn to him in repentance;
• To receive forgiveness;
• To forgive both others and oneself.

The developed ministry of inner healing demands time. It involves prayer that touches on the memories. In a healing service one can make a beginning.

1. Encourage the person to come to the cross in their mind's eye.
2. Encourage them to make an act of forgiving others.
3. Pray for them to be given grace to do so if they cannot.
4. Pray for God's peace to suffuse and hold them.
5. Read assuring passages of the Bible.
6. Continue to pray in silence.
7. Arrange for any further ministry.

Confidentiality is crucial.

Conclusion

Prayer: Collect for peace, *ASB* p 69 para 44. Blessing *ASB* p 145 para 54.

Session 5: Guided by God

Aim

To help participants to be more aware of the guidance that God can give, and to understand the value of gifts of the Spirit in the healing ministry.

Worship

Come down O love divine	AMR 235, MPC 89
Come Holy Ghost	AMR 157, MPC 90
Father I place into your hands	MPC 133, SOFC 97
For this purpose Christ was revealed	MPC 153, SOFC 114
Let your living water flow	SOFC 334
Lift up your heads to the coming King	MPC 418, SOFC 336
Master speak! Thy servant heareth	MPC 459, SOFC 386
Spirit of the living God	MPC 613, SOFC 510
Guide me O Thou great redeemer	AMR 296, MPC 201, SOFC 148

Reading: 1 Samuel 3.1–21.

Prayers: Collects for the guidance of the Holy Spirit, *ASB* p 909 (also CW)

Teaching

God's desire is to make his will known. From the opening chapters of Genesis to the final words of Revelation God shows a desire to reveal himself and to make his will known. He reveals himself through creation (Ps 19.1–4), through his word (Jn 17.7), through the Spirit (Jn 15.26), and pre-eminently through his Son (Heb 1.1–4). The means he employs are manifold:

- the Scriptures (2 Tim. 3.16);
- visions (Acts 10.9–20);
- prophets (2 Sam 12);
- dreams (Matt 1. 18–21);
- human messengers (Neh 1.2–11);
- signs (Exodus 13.21,22);
- angels (Lk 1.11, 26);
- spiritual gifts (1 Cor 12.7–11);
- teaching and preaching (Acts 2.17–40);
- miracles (Rom 15. 19).

Although Christians have always accepted that God may speak to us through the Bible, and through preaching and teaching, there has often been little expectation that God would communicate more immediately in prayer. Some have thought that such things are of the past. Yet the Bible declares that Jesus Christ is the same yesterday, today, and forever (Heb 13.8), that he is alive for evermore (Rev 1. 18), and that he has sent his Spirit upon his church (John 16.13–5). And we are constantly admonished to listen to what the Spirit says.

Many, perhaps most, Christians have at some stage experienced God's particular guidance in the form of a 'spiritual nudge.' Perhaps after receiving communion, we have thought of someone, and later contacted them, only to discover how opportune it was. Or perhaps in private prayer someone comes to mind unexpectedly, and we find out later that there was a great need for prayer.

Exercise
Break into buzz groups of three or four people and discuss: 'Have I been aware in my life of nudges from the Lord, and what form did they take?' Allow a brief opportunity for some report back afterwards.

Spiritual Gifts
Having seen that God does speak today through the operation of his Holy Spirit, we now move on to look at the gifts of the Spirit and their role in the healing ministry. Those that involve some degree of divine guidance are more definite, specific, and ministry orientated than simple 'nudges' or even personal guidance. The classic text for their identity and use is 1 Cor 12–14. The nine spiritual gifts mentioned there can be conveniently classified under three headings:

1. Gifts of Revelation
Word of wisdom; word of knowledge; discernment of spirits.

2. Gifts of Communication
Prophecy; tongues; interpretation.

3. Gifts of Power
Healing; faith; miracles

All of these can have a part to play in healing. Sometimes they are easy to distinguish, at other times they may seem to run into each other.

Word of knowledge: a communication from the Holy Spirit concerning the existence of a specific physical ailment or an inner condition, to which God wishes to bring healing or wholeness (see John 4.16f, the woman at the well in Samaria). The 'word of knowledge' may come in a variety of ways:

i)   Empathetic pain in the part of the body afflicted.
ii) Picture in one's mind of the part of the body concerned.
iii) Picture of incidents in the person's life.
iv) Symbolic pictures, or visual words like a film subtitle.

v) A strong inner impression.
vi) The audible word of God.

Word of wisdom: an immediate inspiration from the Holy Spirit giving insight into a difficult or problematic situation and providing the wisdom as to how best to communicate it. 'The right words to say and the right way of saying them' (see Matt 22.15f, the tribute to Caesar).

Discernment of spirits: a special non-deductive ability God gives to know whether apparent spiritual manifestations or revelations purported to be of God are in reality divine, or whether they are human or even Satanic. There is therefore a link with deliverance. It is not a gift of criticism!

Prophecy: an immediate message from God to his people through an obviously inspired utterance or vision. What is said may offer encouragement to people to seek healing. A picture or a word is received or a phrase or a longer communication. The one who utters it may not always be aware of how relevant it is (see Acts 21.10f, Rev 1.9–20).

Tongues: this is a prayer gift. When used privately it often helps in instances where we are not certain how to pray. Used in ministry it frequently triggers off the other gifts—knowledge, wisdom or prophecy via interpretation (see Acts 2.4f, 10.46, 19.6).

Interpretation: not the same as a translation. The gift of interpretation conveys the meaning that God wishes to communicate through a prior speaking in tongues. It may be experienced as a picture, as a word or words. It may express a deep felt prayer, an act of praise, or be in fact a word of knowledge, wisdom, or prophecy.

Miracles: miracles other than those of healing seem to be what is meant (see Mk 6.13f, 45f ; Jn 11.38; Acts 13.11).

Faith: the special gift of faith (the faith that 'moves mountains') is something more than the faith all of us need to be saved. It is not only a great trust in God, but also a knowing that he is going to do something—which then happens. In relationship to the healing ministry, this gift of faith might enable someone to say 'You are healed' (and it happens), and not the normal 'May you be healed' (see Matt 17.20, Lk 13.12, Acts 3.6).

Healing: strictly *gifts* (plural) of healing. All of us are called upon to pray for one another that we may be healed but God gives to some, as a focus of the ministry of all, specific gifts of healing, whereby they seem to be noticeably used by God in particular aspects of the Christian healing ministry.

The Group: A Testing Place

When we realize how God can guide us through the use of the gifts of the Spirit, and how they help to communicate his healing love in Jesus, then we can understand why Paul urges us to 'set our hearts' on them (1 Cor 14.1). They are not prizes or badges of spiritual merit, but tools for ministry. They are intended for the upbuilding of the body of Christ and the extension of the kingdom of God. They are available now, through prayer, as we ask God to equip us all for ministry in his name.

While encouraging us to ask for the gifts of the Spirit, and warning against quenching the Spirit, Paul is also concerned that any apparent spiritual gifts should be tested, and that their public use should be orderly (1 Thess 5.19–22; 1 Cor 14.39–49). The small group is once more the place where we can learn. In this setting the gifts can be fostered and tested. Three things are needed: (a) an openness to the gifts; (b) a readiness to try them out; and (c) a preparedness to be wrong.

What will often happen is that as those who have the gift of tongues are allowed to use it, others become more aware of God's presence. This opens the door firstly to an interpretation, and then to a more independent manifestation of various gifts, as well as to guidance in general.

Many of the 'revelations' that are shared will meet with confirmation by others saying 'it feels right.' Or they may have had the same vision or word. In a ministering situation the person can usually be expected to express recognition. If the revelation is directional or predictive, however, there needs to be a much more stringent testing:

1. Does it accord with the Bible?
2. Does it accord with basic Christian teaching?
3. Does it convey a sense of God's presence?
4. Is it fundamentally conducive to love, joy, and peace?
5. Does the person expressing it live a trustworthy life?
6. Is their ministry proven?
7. Is there any other confirmation?

When we are learning how to use the gifts, it is important not to seem to claim an authority we do not yet possess. If we feel God has given us a revelation, we should put it out to test, by beginning 'It seems to me God is saying…' or 'Does this mean anything to you?' rather than 'Thus says the Lord!'

Comments and Cautions

- You must have renounced and be cleansed of any occult involvement.
- Beware of pride if God seems to be using you.
- Beware of jealousy of others' gifts.
- Beware of a judgmental or critical attitude.
- Always respect the person being ministered to.

Testimony

The testimony is to a healing following the exercise of gifts of the Spirit. Gerry is known to her friends as a very matter-of-fact sort of person. She came to a healing service curious, but sceptical. A married woman in her 40s, she had been growing in faith, and had come to confirmation. She still had many questions, particularly about the power of God today, and had been suffering all day from an acute pain in the back of the neck. During the service the Holy Spirit was called upon in prayer. Then a member of the visiting team said that God knew there was someone present suffering from acute pain in a specific part of the neck, and was wanting to heal him or her. Her friends persuaded her to go forward. She was the only person to respond to this particular word of knowledge. Two people prayed for her and she felt a warm sensation and the pain went. She spontaneously shouted aloud, 'Oh! It's gone!' This experience has helped to strengthen her faith, and to confirm that God is real and active in the world today.

Workshop

Mention the aim of the session and briefly summarize the main points of the teaching. Then pray with and for each other in groups, as before. Give time to invoking the Holy Spirit and trying to discern his inspiration. Pray as the Spirit seems to lead you. Allow those who may have the gift of tongues to use it. Share any revelation that seems to come. Test its relevance.

Summary of Teaching

- God desires to make his will known.
- He reveals himself in Jesus.
- He uses many means through the Spirit—Bible, teaching, people, dreams, prayer.
- The common experience of 'spiritual nudges.'
- Being helped by God's Spirit in the healing ministry.
- The nine spiritual gifts mentioned in 1 Cor 12:
  (a) *Gifts of Revelation:* word of wisdom, word of knowledge, discernment of spirits.
  (b) *Gifts of Communication:* prophecy, tongues, interpretation.
  (c) *Gifts of Power* healing, faith, miracles.
- Such gifts are not badges of merit, but tools for ministry—available now, through prayer.
- The group as a testing place.
- Three things needed:
  (a) an openness to the gifts;
  (b) a readiness to try them out;
  (c) a preparedness to be wrong.

Conclusion

Prayer: Collect for the church's witness, *ASB* p 258 para 88. The Grace.

Session 6: Putting it Together

Aim

To make the participants aware of essential considerations needed in order to decide what style of healing ministry is right for their own context, and to introduce them to more public ministry in teams.

Worship

Crown him with many crowns	AMR 224, MPC 109, SOFC 77
From heaven you came	MPC 162, SOFC 120
I, the Lord of sea and sky	SOF2 830
Lift high the Cross	AMR 633, MPC 417
Majesty, worship his majesty	MPC 454, SOFC 379
Thou Lord, hast given thyself for our healing	MPC 698
Praise to the Lord, the almighty	AMR 382, MPC 564, SOFC 470
Praise you, Lord, for the wonder of your healing	MPC 565, SOFC 472

Reading: Mark 5.21–42.

Prayer: Collect for Epiphany 5, *ASB* p 480 (also CW Trinity 1).

Lord's Prayer.

Teaching

Wisdom in the Healing Ministry of Jesus and his Apostles

Jesus carried out his ministry of healing in a variety of ways. He publicly healed in the synagogue, during an act of worship. He healed people after teaching and praying. Great groups of people came to him, and he went to individuals. Some of what he did was completely in the public eye; at other times it was more private. Both his own mission and the needs of the individual had to be considered. In the story of the restoration to life of Jairus' daughter there are a number of important points. On one hand it involves the woman with a haemorrhage being healed and having this made very public. On the other hand, when he reaches Jairus' house he does not let anyone come in with him to minister except the child's parents and only three of the apostles: Peter, James, and John. Part of this clearly had to do with the need not be perturbed by the lack of faith of the people gathered at the house, and to have supportive people with him. An appropriate setting was needed for such a difficult ministry.

In the ministry of the apostles after Pentecost there are the healings that take place through chance encounters, when they minister then and there—as with the lame man at the beautiful gate of the temple. There are the crowds who come to them seeking healing (Acts 5.12–16). While Paul is preaching, his glance falls upon the man at Lystra who has been lame from birth, sees he has faith and orders him to be well (Acts 14.8f). The discussion in 1 Cor 12–14 indicates that gifts of the Spirit relevant to healing were being regularly used in public worship.

One thing is very clear. In the apostolic church there was plenty of opportunity to receive the ministry of healing, and a variety of ways in which it happened.

Options

There are a number of options for a parish wishing to move forward in the ministry of healing by involving lay people in a more personal fashion. They include:

1. What Service?

a) *Private?* Using the team in ministry in homes, hospitals or in church, normally prearranged. Here, a set service may or may not be used.

b) *Eucharistic?* The ministry takes place in the service of Holy Communion.

c) *Office?* The ministry takes place in the context of either morning or evening prayer.

d) *Special?* The ministry takes place in the context of a specially designed act of worship.

2. Where in the Service Should General Ministry Take Place?

a) *In the middle?* This is particularly suitable if it is known that only a small number of people will receive ministry. Time is restricted.

b) *After the service?* This has the great advantage of allowing time, but it is not as corporate. Others leaving may disturb the praying.

c) *At the end?* This is done by beginning the ministry before the end of the service. The congregation join in devotional singing, or silent prayer as people come forward for ministry. The service is officially concluded with a blessing, allowing people to leave, while the ministry and some worship continues. Or (at the Eucharist), people may go straight from receiving communion to be prayed with in a chapel or such like.

3. What Method?

a) *Simple invitation?* People are given a clear invitation to come forward to receive ministry, which is being offered in the sanctuary, or other designated area. This does not preclude going unobtrusively up to people who may be staying behind and asking if they would like ministry.

b) *Open ministry?* The ministering team(s) go about praying with those who desire it. This may be suitable in open air situations or where there are very large numbers. It is often linked with the 'open' use of certain gifts of the Spirit (when attention must be given to questions of order and authenticity).

4. Is the Ministry to Include Anointing with Oil?

This is generally seen as a more solemn ministry. Is it to be available as an option during more informal ministry? The actual anointing is done by a priest or other authorized minister, usually using set forms of prayer. This does not exclude more extempore prayer surrounding it.

5. How is the Venue to be Used?

Where will the ministry take place? Will there be sufficient privacy? Will people be expected to kneel, sit, or stand? Is there a place for more intensive ministry, where people can sit? Will the temperature be warm enough? Is there to be music during the time of ministry? Of what sort?

6. If the Ministry is to Take Place During a 'Special' Service, What Style of Worship Will There Be?

Will it reflect the normal style ('free' or 'formal' or both, 'visual,' with candles and colour, or plain or in-between, popular or traditional or mixed musically)? If not, why not?

7. How Often?

Once a month is probably a minimum for any regular ministry (with a possible gap in summer and at Christmas). In addition special services may have their place during parish missions or other evangelistic campaigns, and on ecumenical occasions. The option of ministry at a small weekday service may help those who need 'soaking' prayer. Flexibility is important, taking seriously the particular needs of a personal situation.

Introducing It

1. Prepare the congregation beforehand with teaching and discussion.
2. The first time such ministry is made available, the service at which it takes place will need to have a specific focus on healing.
3. Any advertisement should make clear that what is being offered is a *Christian* ministry.
4. Local doctors will often appreciate being told of what is happening, and its nature.
5. The team(s) must be prepared.

The Healing Group and the Ministering Teams

Ministering teams comprise two or three people. The ministering group is the body that includes all those ministering. It is helpful to have Christian doctors or nurses in the group, though boundaries need to be observed during ministry (which is not an opportunity for a free consultation).

Acceptance of authority is crucial. The final word as to who is allowed to minister publicly, and what style of ministry is offered, belongs to the priest or pastor. No one should be permitted to take part in this ministry unless they are

30

faithful and committed Christians, as far as they are aware, living in a state of grace. Particular care needs to be taken to see that there is no-one involved in the healing group who has any unrenounced occult involvement. Individuals should prepare themselves beforehand for ministry by self-examination, and prayer, and try to arrive in an undistracted state. Fasting and vigil may be an important part of individual or corporate preparation, or follow-up. It is inadvisable to be fasting on the day itself.

Even if it meets at other times, the healing group should meet for a short time of prayer just before each service at which ministry is to be offered. This should include:

- Silent self-examination and repentance;
- Reconciliation if necessary.;
- Prayer for each other, perhaps with laying on of hands;
- Prayer for the service and all involved in leading it;
- Prayer that God would draw those he wishes to come;
- Prayer for all who will be present;
- Prayer for spiritual protection.

While observing confidences, an informal review after ministering (in teams or as a group or both) will be found helpful, as will an occasional general review.

Comments and Cautions
- Be prepared for experiencing a process of healing and sanctification within oneself and within the group.
- Be prepared for criticism. Some will be justified, some not; weigh it and evaluate it.
- The reality of grace can be disturbing. Be prepared for unexpected and irrational hostility. Meet it with understanding, love, and reason.
- Be prepared for the occasional deeper awareness of spiritual conflict. Call on the name of Jesus, and hand it over to him.

Workshop
(a) Divide into groups. Discuss what style of ministry might be most appropriate in your own local situation.
(b) The culmination of the course is an experience of ministering, and being ministered to, in an 'invitation ministry' style. First, each group prays briefly as suggested below under 'Group Preparation.' Then each group divides into teams of two or three.

When invited, everyone comes forward to a designated station for ministry — asking at least for some simple blessing. The first set of teams begins to minister. After they have prayed with two or three people, the teams are replaced, so that everyone has an opportunity both to minister and to receive ministry.

Summary of Teaching
- Wisdom shown by Jesus and the apostles in their healing ministry.
- Plenty of opportunity and a variety of ways. Options and considerations:
  ◊ At what occasion (private, eucharistic, office, special)?
  ◊ At what point?
  ◊ In what way ('invitation' or 'open,' with anointing)?
  ◊ How often?
  ◊ With what style of worship?
  ◊ How will the venue be used?
  ◊ Will those seeking ministry kneel, sit, or stand?
  ◊ Will there be enough privacy?
  ◊ Will there be a place for more intensive ministry?
  ◊ What are the possibilities for further ministry?
  ◊ How is it going to be introduced and advertised?
- The healing group and teams: membership, meetings, reviews.
- Individual preparation: repentance, prayer, fasting, vigil.
- Group preparation prior to ministry:
  ◊ silent self-examination and repentance;
  ◊ reconciliation if necessary;
  ◊ prayer for each other, perhaps with laying on of hands;
  ◊ prayer for the service and all involved in leading it;
  ◊ prayer that God would draw those he wishes to come;
  ◊ prayer for all who will receive ministry;
  ◊ prayer for all who will be present;
  ◊ prayer for spiritual protection.

Conclusion
Prayers: Ascription, *ASB* p 107 para 16. Blessing, *ASB* p 107 para 19.